DEADLY DISEASES

THE BUBONIC PLAGUE

BY YVETTE LaPIERRE

CONTENT CONSULTANT
Viveka Vadyvaloo
Associate Professor
Washington State University

Core Library

An Imprint of Abdo Publishing

Cover image: The bubonic plague is caused by tiny bacteria that
spread through infected fleas.

abdobooks.com

Published by Abdo Publishing, a division of ABDO, PO Box 398166, Minneapolis, Minnesota 55439. Copyright © 2022 by Abdo Consulting Group, Inc. International copyrights reserved in all countries. No part of this book may be reproduced in any form without written permission from the publisher. Core Library™ is a trademark and logo of Abdo Publishing.

Printed in the United States of America, North Mankato, Minnesota.
102021
012022

THIS BOOK CONTAINS
RECYCLED MATERIALS

Cover Photo: Kateryna Kon/Shutterstock Images
Interior Photos: Eye of Science/Science Source, 4–5, 43; Everett Collection/Shutterstock Images, 7; Gallinago Media/Shutterstock Images, 10; New York Public Library/Science Source, 12–13, 45; Michal Szymanski/Shutterstock Images, 15; Jean-Loup Charmet/Science Source, 17; SPL/Science Source, 19; Tim Vernon/Science Source, 22–23; American Philosophical Society/Science Source, 25; Science Source, 28; Shutterstock Images, 30, 36; Jack Dempsey/AP Images, 32–33; David Zalubowski/AP Images, 35; Red Line Editorial, 39

Editor: Arnold Ringstad
Series Designer: Ryan Gale

Library of Congress Control Number: 2021941237

Publisher's Cataloging-in-Publication Data

Names: LaPierre, Yvette, author.
Title: The bubonic plague / by Yvette LaPierre
Description: Minneapolis, Minnesota : Abdo Publishing, 2022 | Series: Deadly diseases | Includes
    online resources and index.
Identifiers: ISBN 9781532196560 (lib. bdg.) | ISBN 9781098218379 (ebook)
Subjects: LCSH: Bubonic plague--Juvenile literature. | Black Death--Juvenile literature. | Plague--
    History--Juvenile literature. | Infectious diseases--Juvenile literature. | Epidemics--History--
    Juvenile literature. | Communicable diseases--Epidemiology--Juvenile literature.
Classification: DDC 614.49--dc23

CONTENTS

CHAPTER ONE
A Terrifying Disease **4**

CHAPTER TWO
**The History of
the Bubonic Plague** **12**

CHAPTER THREE
**The Science of
the Bubonic Plague** **22**

CHAPTER FOUR
Treating the Bubonic Plague **32**

Important Dates **42**

Stop and Think **44**

Glossary **46**

Online Resources **47**

Learn More **47**

Index **48**

About the Author **48**

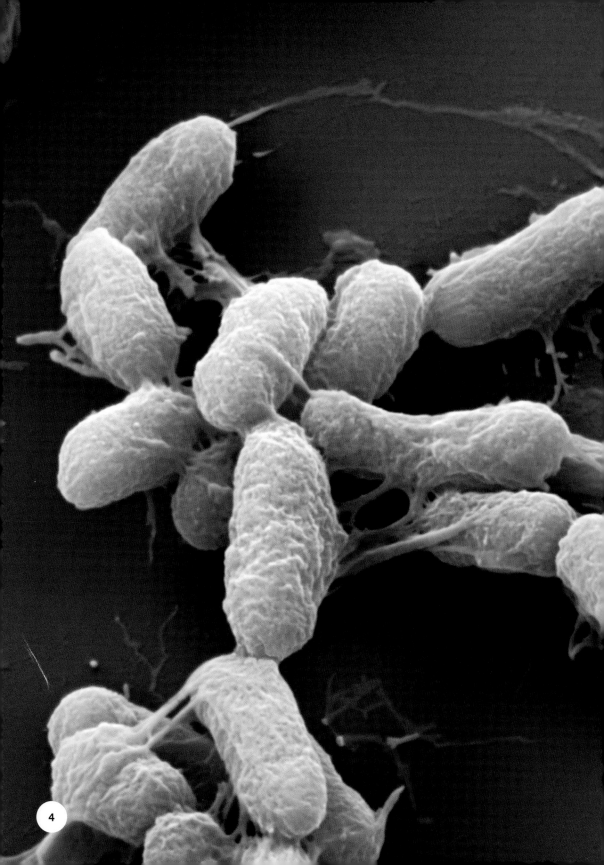

4

A TERRIFYING DISEASE

On an October day in 1347, Italian merchant ships sailed into the harbor of Messina, Sicily. Dockworkers gathered. They were ready to unload spices, silks, and other goods from East Asia. Instead they found ships full of dead and dying sailors. Those still alive suffered from high fevers and pain. They were covered in black spots and huge swellings that oozed blood and pus. Officials quickly ordered the ships to

The people of the 1300s had no way of knowing that tiny bacteria were responsible for the frightening bubonic plague.

turn around. But it was too late. The ships had already delivered the mysterious disease to Europe.

PERSPECTIVES
"BLESS YOU!"

The Roman Empire was struck by an early bubonic plague epidemic. In 590 CE, the disease reached Rome. Many people believed the disease was sent by God. They also believed God could end the plague. The pope at the time ordered people to pray to halt the disease. People began saying "God bless you" if someone sneezed. Sneezing was thought to be an early symptom of plague. The phrase was meant to cure the person and stop the spread of plague. The phrase caught on. Many people still say "Bless you!" when someone sneezes today.

Even before the ships arrived, Europeans had heard rumors about a terrible disease. They didn't know what it was or what caused it. But they knew it was deadly. Once it arrived, it quickly spread throughout Europe. In just five years, the terrifying disease killed more than 20 million Europeans.

Art from the 1400s shows the boils and swellings, or buboes, caused by the bubonic plague.

THE BUBONIC PLAGUE

This disease is now known as the bubonic plague. It is caused by bacteria called *Yersinia pestis*. *Y. pestis* can grow in many rodents, such as marmots, rats, and squirrels. The disease spreads from animal to animal, mostly through the bite of fleas. It can kill animals just as it can people. Occasionally the fleas bite humans and cause a serious infection.

The bacteria cause lymph nodes to swell. These large, painful swellings are called buboes. The word was used in the Middle Ages. That's why the disease became known as the bubonic plague.

The bubonic plague is one of the deadliest diseases in human history. It has been with humanity since ancient times. Scientists now believe the bubonic plague first appeared in Asia thousands of years ago. From there, it spread around the world. It was likely carried by rats and their fleas onto trading caravans and ships.

The plague is responsible for some of the most terrifying pandemics the world has ever seen. The most infamous is now known as the Black Death. This pandemic happened in the 1300s CE. The sickness spread from China to the Middle East and Africa. It then reached Europe on ships. By the time the pandemic ended, as much as one-third of Europe's population was dead. The final bubonic plague pandemic struck in the late 1800s and early 1900s. It reached the United States in 1900. This global outbreak killed more than 10 million people.

THE BUBONIC PLAGUE TODAY

The bubonic plague is not a thing of the past. *Y. pestis* can still be found around the world in wild rodents and their fleas. However, cases in humans are relatively rare now. A few thousand cases are reported worldwide each year. More than 90 percent of cases

ZOONOSIS

The bubonic plague is an example of a zoonosis. A zoonosis is an infectious disease that passes from animals to humans. The World Health Organization (WHO) estimates that more than 60 percent of current human diseases came from animals. In addition, most new diseases that appear in the world are from animals. Research suggests that overpopulation, climate change, and humans taking over wild habitats have led to more cases of zoonosis.

In some places, such as Madagascar, the plague can still be found in rats.

occur in Africa. The United States reports about seven cases each year.

The plague is not as deadly as it used to be, either. Public health efforts have rid most cities of infected rats. Doctors now have a clear understanding of what causes the plague. They know how to diagnose and treat the disease and prevent large-scale outbreaks.

STRAIGHT TO THE
SOURCE

The Italian writer Giovanni Boccaccio was an eyewitness to the Black Death in Florence, Italy. In 1350, he wrote *The Decameron*. It is a long and detailed description of the devastating plague:

> *The city was full of corpses. The dead were usually given the same treatment by their neighbors. . . . They would drag the corpse out of the home and place it in front of the doorstep, where, usually in the morning, quantities of dead bodies could be seen by any passerby. . . . So many corpses would arrive in front of a church every day and at every hour that the amount of holy ground for burials was certainly insufficient for the ancient custom of giving each body its individual place; when all the graves were full, huge trenches were dug in all of the cemeteries of the churches and into them the new arrivals were dumped by the hundreds.*

Source: Giovanni Boccaccio. *The Decameron*, trans. Mark Musa and Peter Bondanella. W.W. Norton, 1982.

BACK IT UP

The author of this passage is using evidence to support a point. Write a sentence describing the point the author is making. Then write down two or three pieces of evidence the author uses to make the point.

THE HISTORY OF THE BUBONIC PLAGUE

The bubonic plague is an ancient disease. It may have struck ancient Egypt thousands of years ago. Writings describe patients suffering from diseases with black spots and lumps. It's possible the plague was mentioned in the Bible, too. The Old Testament mentions an illness with similar symptoms to those of the bubonic plague.

New research suggests that the plague is more than 3,000 years old. *Y. pestis* may have

Artwork showing the plague pandemics of the past often features grim imagery, such as skeletons and bodies being carried away.

PLAGUE ORIGINS

Experts long debated where the plague started and when. They relied on historical accounts of epidemics for answers. Now they have scientific evidence. In 2011, a team of scientists studied bones in a mass grave from the Black Death. They found DNA from *Y. pestis*. Other scientists then found more of the bacterial DNA in ancient skeletons. They compared the older DNA with that found in *Y. pestis* today. The DNA evidence suggests that the plague is more than 3,000 years old. It may have started in marmots in the Tian Shan mountains in Asia.

first appeared in an area of central China. It spread from there to Egypt and beyond. That strain of *Y. pestis* caused multiple devastating pandemics.

THE PLAGUE OF JUSTINIAN

The first recorded bubonic plague pandemic hit Egypt in the 500s CE. Trade caravans and ships carried infected animals and fleas. Plague spread from central China to Egypt in 541. At the time, the Byzantine Empire controlled much of the region. This empire was

The emperor Justinian I, *center*, was in charge during one of history's first famous bubonic plague pandemics.

ruled by Justinian I. The pandemic is now known as the Justinian Plague.

The plague spread to the busy capital city of Constantinople in 542. According to a historian of the time, as many as 10,000 people a day died from the plague. The pandemic ravaged much of the Middle East, North Africa, Asia, and Europe. It finally ended in 767.

THE BLACK DEATH

The most famous plague pandemic is the one now known as the Black Death. It overwhelmed Europe beginning in the 1300s. More people died of the plague than in all the wars of that era. Experts estimate that as many as 25 to 30 million people died in Europe. That was about one-third of the continent's population. It took 200 years for the population to recover.

The plague spread along trade routes from East Asia. Infected rats and their fleas rode aboard caravans and ships. The plague reached Italy in 1347. From there, it raced across Europe and wiped out entire towns. Terrified people fled to the countryside, spreading it further. They abandoned homes and even their families. By New Year's Day in 1349, 200 people were dying every day in London. The bodies piled up so quickly that they were buried in mass graves.

Plague victims first had high fevers, headaches, and chills. Then came the painful swellings in armpits, necks,

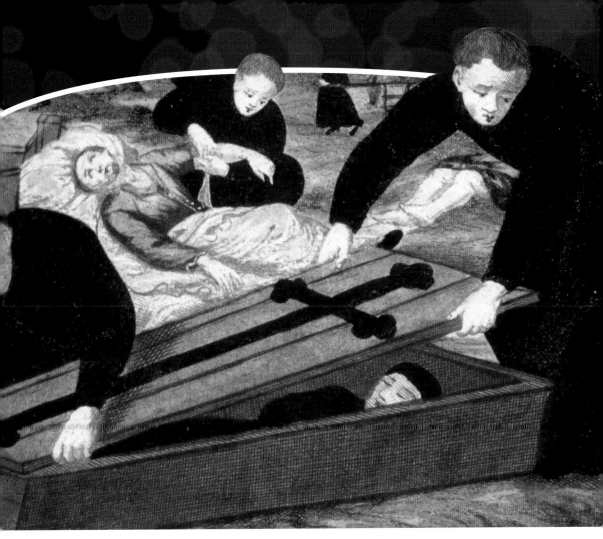

Doctors tried to help people during the Black Death, but their methods did not work.

or groins. Skin and sores turned black. That's how the pandemic got the name Black Death. After three or four days of suffering, most people died. Some dropped dead in the middle of the road. Others died in the fields. Crops were left unharvested. Livestock ran free.

An Italian historian even died in the middle of writing a sentence.

Europeans didn't know what this frightening disease was. They didn't know what caused it or how to treat it. Some thought the disease was sent by God as a punishment. Many thought it was caused by poisonous air. Doctors cut open and drained the buboes. They prescribed bloodletting, vomiting, and sweating. They thought that this would release the poisons. They even strapped live chickens to the buboes as a cure.

Epidemics of plague continued over the next three centuries. The disease struck countries and cities throughout Europe. An outbreak in England in 1361 was called the children's plague. It killed mostly young people. The disease continued to spread in European countries in the 1600s. Almost 70,000 people died in London from 1665 to 1666 in the Great Plague. In 1720, as many as 40,000 people died in an outbreak in France. After that, the plague seemed to mostly disappear.

THE BLACK DEATH
IN EUROPE

This map shows how the Black Death came to Europe and spread. What path did it take through Europe? What parts of Europe did the plague reach first? What parts were infected last?

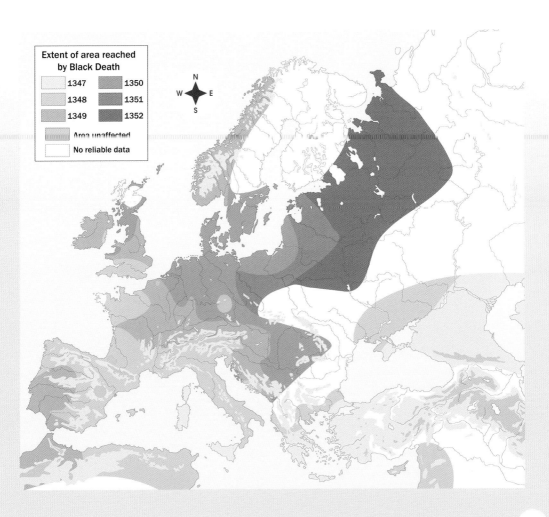

Extent of area reached
by Black Death

1347	1350
1348	1351
1349	1352

Area unaffected

No reliable data

N
W E
S

The poet Petrarch lived during the Black Death in Italy. He imagined a future when people wouldn't believe such a terrible plague happened. He wrote: "O happy posterity, who will not experience such abysmal woe and will look upon our testimony as a fable."

THE MODERN PLAGUE

The final bubonic plague pandemic is called the Manchurian or Modern Plague. Experts think it started in southwestern China in the 1850s. It spread along railways. It moved from port city to port city. By the early 1900s, the disease had spread to every continent except Antarctica. In the United States, outbreaks hit San Francisco, California, in 1900 and Pensacola, Florida, in 1922. It was the most widespread of all the plague pandemics.

Like all bubonic plague pandemics, it created fear and confusion. But it also resulted in scientific advancements. The pandemic helped scientists finally discover the true cause of the bubonic plague.

EXPLORE ONLINE

Chapter Two discusses the bubonic plague pandemic known as the Black Death. The website below explores the causes and effects of the deadly plague. How is the information from the website the same as the information in Chapter Two? What new information did you learn? Why is it important to study diseases from long ago?

THE PAST, PRESENT, AND FUTURE OF THE BUBONIC PLAGUE

abdocorelibrary.com/the-bubonic-plague

THE SCIENCE OF THE BUBONIC PLAGUE

When the final plague pandemic began in the 1800s, the disease was still a mystery. Doctors did not know what caused it. They did not know how to treat it. But by this time, scientists had learned a lot about diseases in general. In the late 1800s, researchers proved that tiny living things could cause disease. That included bacteria. This idea became known as germ theory. It replaced the old idea that poisonous air or evil spirits made

Not until the late 1800s did scientists discover that tiny fleas spread even tinier bacteria to cause the bubonic plague.

people sick. Armed with this new knowledge, scientists could finally solve the mystery of the plague.

SCIENTIFIC BREAKTHROUGHS

In 1894 an outbreak of the bubonic plague struck Hong Kong. Two different biologists decided to look for the cause. One was a Swiss-French scientist named Alexandre Yersin. The other was Kitasato Shibasaburo of Japan. Each took samples of fluids from plague victims. They found bacteria in the samples. Then they injected the bacteria into healthy animals. The animals got sick and died of plague. The biologists had found the bacterium that causes the bubonic plague. This bacterium was later named *Yersinia pestis*.

Researchers found that *Y. pestis* lives in certain rodents. Fleas spread the bacteria from animal to animal. The tropical rat flea does the best job of spreading plague. Its scientific name is *Xenopsylla cheopis*. The flea bites a rat infected with plague

Kitasato Shibasaburo was a pioneer in the study of bacteria.

DEMONS AND SUPERSTITIONS

Before *Y. pestis* was discovered in the late 1800s, people developed many theories to explain the plague. An earthquake that spewed poisonous air was one explanation.

Doctors in Paris, France, blamed the alignment of planets on March 20, 1345. In Messina, Italy, people believed the plague was carried by demons in the shape of black dogs. Scandinavians thought a Pest Maiden emerged like a blue flame from a dead person. It flew to the next victim. In Lithuania, people believed that the Pest Maiden waved a red scarf through a door or window to let in the disease.

bacteria. It drinks rat blood filled with *Y. pestis*. The bacteria multiply inside the flea. They begin to block the flea's gut. When the flea bites another animal, it can't digest the new blood. Instead, it spits blood and bacteria into the new animal. The flea is now starving. It bites again and again, increasing the chance to spread plague bacteria.

PLAGUE IN NATURE

The bubonic plague mostly affects small

wild animals. Rabbits, squirrels, rats, marmots, and other rodents in certain areas carry *Y. pestis*. They are called host animals. In these populations, plague is enzootic. That means it's always present in at least a few animals.

Usually only a few animals in a population are infected at a time. Infected animals may not get sick and die. Fleas can still bite an infected animal and get bacteria from its blood. Then they can pass the bacteria to an uninfected animal. Sometimes this natural cycle goes out of control. When that happens, humans are at risk.

PLAGUE IN HUMANS

Sometimes the plague becomes epizootic. That means it affects a lot of host animals in a population. This may happen because of a change in the environment or climate. During an epizootic cycle, lots of host animals die. The hungry fleas look for other living hosts. They might bite and infect cats, dogs, and humans.

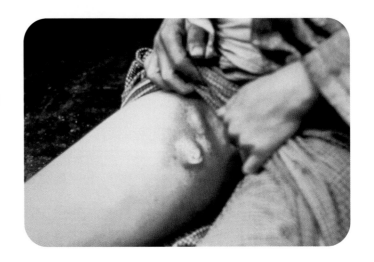

In a person with the bubonic plague, swollen lymph nodes can be seen through the skin.

Plague in humans has three forms. The first form is the bubonic plague. The bacteria invade lymph nodes. After a couple of days, the nodes swell. The swollen nodes become painful. Eventually they may turn black. Other symptoms include fever, chills, and headache. Victims often feel very tired.

People can get the bubonic plague from flea bites or from handling infected animals. The bubonic plague is the most common disease caused by *Y. pestis*. It is also the least deadly today, because it is easily treated. If left untreated, it can kill victims within a few days. It also can spread to other parts of the body. However, the bubonic plague can't spread from person to person.

The second form happens when *Y. pestis* spreads to blood. This is called septicemic plague. Septicemia is also known as blood poisoning. Sometimes flea bites spread this form of plague. Early symptoms are similar to those of the bubonic plague. They include fever, chills, and pain. This form of plague doesn't cause buboes. Instead, internal bleeding causes dark

PERSPECTIVES

QUARANTINES AND MASKS

During the COVID-19 pandemic that began in 2020, many people wore face masks to protect themselves. If they were sick, they stayed away from others. These protection measures were not new. During the Black Death, Italian officials made sailors stay on their ships for 40 days in case they were carrying the plague. Some cities locked plague victims into their houses for 40 days. The practice is known as quarantine. This word is based on the Italian word for "forty." During the Modern Plague, people covered their mouths and noses with folded cotton. They held the cotton in place with long pieces of gauze that went around their ears. These face coverings helped fight the spread of the pneumonic plague.

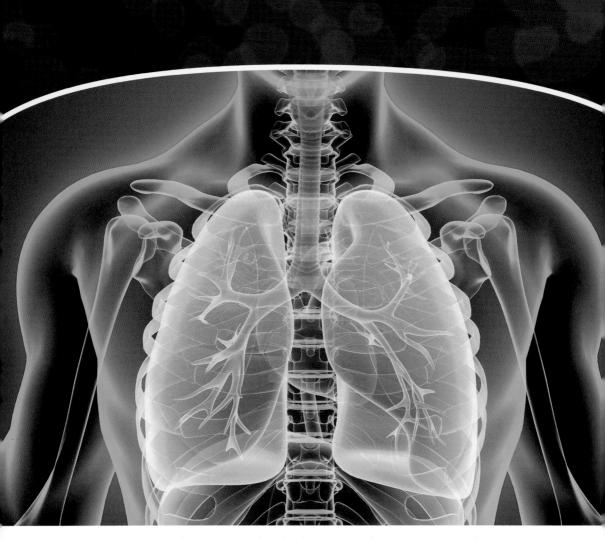

Pneumonic plague attacks the lungs, making it especially dangerous.

patches on the skin. Skin and other tissues turn black

and die. This happens mainly on fingers, toes, and

noses. If untreated, it leads to organ failure and death.

Plague also can invade the lungs. This is the third

form. It is called pneumonic plague. The symptoms are

similar to those of pneumonia. Victims suffer from fever and weakness. They experience chest pain, coughing, and difficulty breathing.

Pneumonic plague is the most dangerous form. It also is the only form that can be spread directly from person to person. An infected person might cough or sneeze. Droplets containing *Y. pestis* can spread in the air. Another person may breathe in the droplets and become infected.

FURTHER EVIDENCE

Chapter Three covers how the plague occurs in nature. It explains how humans get infected. What evidence does the author include? The website at the link below discusses the spread of plague in the United States. Does the website support the evidence provided in the chapter? Does it present new evidence?

PLAGUE ECOLOGY IN THE UNITED STATES

abdocorelibrary.com/the-bubonic-plague

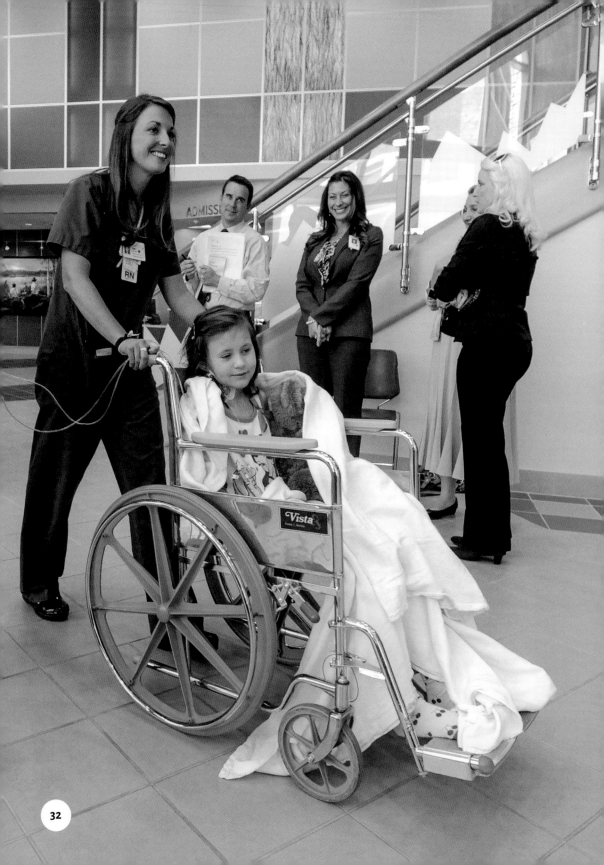

TREATING THE BUBONIC PLAGUE

The bubonic plague still exists in many parts of the world. Most rodent populations that carry the plague are in rural areas with few people. Occasionally, though, cases in humans are reported. These outbreaks are rare and not as alarming as in the past. Advances in diagnosis and treatment mean that the bubonic plague is rarely fatal anymore.

A young girl in Colorado survived bubonic plague in 2012. Doctors believed she was infected by touching a dead squirrel.

33

DIAGNOSING PLAGUE

The most common sign of the bubonic plague is a very swollen and painful lymph node. If the patient has been bitten by a flea recently, plague is a possibility. A doctor also may suspect plague if the patient lives in an area where plague is endemic.

A lab test is needed to confirm the diagnosis. A doctor takes a sample of pus from a bubo, if it is present. For septicemic or pneumonic plague, samples of blood or spit are taken. Lab experts test the sample for the presence of *Y. pestis*. Early diagnosis can save lives.

TREATING PLAGUE

The bubonic plague is a serious disease. However, it can be easily treated. Patients who seek treatment early can expect a full recovery. That's why early diagnosis is key.

Signs may warn the public about a risk of plague in a certain area.

PLAGUE WARNING!!!

<u>Bubonic Plague</u> is an infectious disease which was once referred to as *"The Black Death"*. Prairie dogs and other wild rodents in this area may be infected with PLAGUE. PLAGUE may be transmitted to humans through contact with infected animals or their fleas.

1. STAY OUT AREAS THAT PRAIRIE DOGS INHABIT.
2. AVOID ALL CONTACT WITH PRAIRIE DOGS AND OTHER WILD RODENTS.
3. DO NOT FEED OR PLAY WITH PRAIRIE DOGS.
4. AVOID FLEAS: PROTECT PETS WITH FLEA POWDER, AND KEEP PETS ON A LEASH.
5. DO NOT TOUCH SICK OR DEAD ANIMALS.
6. SEE A PHYSICIAN IF YOU BECOME ILL WITHIN ONE WEEK OF YOUR VISIT TO THIS AREA. PLAGUE IS A TREATABLE ILLNESS.

Tri-County Health Department
15400 E. 14th Place, Suite 309
Aurora, CO 80011
(303) 341-9370

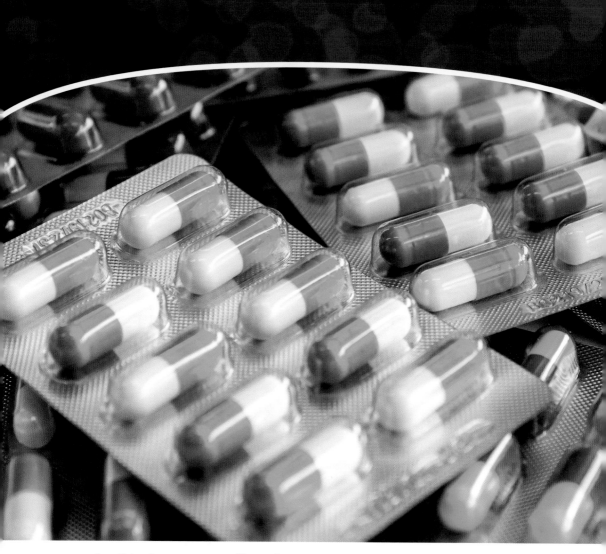

Antibiotics were totally unknown to the people who lived through historical plague pandemics. Today these drugs can cure the bubonic plague.

Because the plague is caused by bacteria, it can be treated with antibiotics. These are medicines that treat bacterial infections. They kill the bacteria or stop them from multiplying.

Early diagnosis helps stop the spread of pneumonic plague. The patient is quickly isolated from others. People who have been in contact with the patient are watched closely. They may be given antibiotics just in case.

Vaccines that protect against the plague have been developed. They have been used in places where people are likely to be exposed to fleas carrying *Y. pestis.* Current plague vaccines aren't very effective, however. The World Health Organization (WHO) recommends them only for people at a high risk for catching plague.

ANTIBIOTIC RESISTANCE

Antibiotics treat bacterial infections, including the plague. Sometimes bacteria evolve ways to protect themselves from the drugs designed to kill them. They become antibiotic resistant. In 2019 two strains of *Y. pestis* were found to be antibiotic resistant. Both strains are in Madagascar. If these strains infect animals in other countries, antibiotic resistant plague could spread.

THE PLAGUE TODAY

Plague exists on every continent in the world except Antarctica and in the region of Oceania, which consists of thousands of islands including Australia and New Zealand. Many human cases reported in recent decades have been in rural areas. The plague is no longer only a disease of cities. It appears in small villages and farming areas too.

From 2010 to 2015, 3,248 cases of plague were reported in people worldwide. Of those cases, 584 people died. Most human cases since the 1990s have occurred in Africa. The three countries that report the most cases are the Democratic Republic of the Congo, Madagascar, and Peru.

The plague first reached the United States in 1900. Rat-infested ships brought it to San Francisco. It spread from there. In 1924 Los Angeles had a plague epidemic. That was the last outbreak in an urban area in the United States. Since then, the disease has spread to

WORLDWIDE PLAGUE CASES

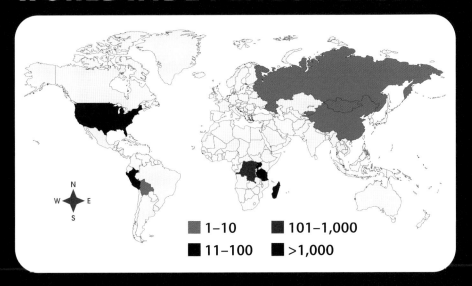

■ 1–10	■ 101–1,000
■ 11–100	■ >1,000

This map shows the total reported cases of human plague in several countries between 2013 and 2018. Which parts of the world have no reported cases of plague? Which have the most cases of plague? Why do you think that might be?

rural areas in western states. It occurs in voles, squirrels, rabbits, kangaroo rats, and other rodents. These animals live in grasslands and scrub woodlands of states such as Arizona, Colorado, New Mexico, and Utah.

Since 2000 the United States has had an average of seven cases of human plague a year. More than 80 percent of cases are the bubonic form. Most are the result of a flea bite or handling an infected animal.

PERSPECTIVES

PLAGUE AS A WEAPON

During World War II (1939–1945), the Japanese military researched the use of the bubonic plague as a bioweapon. It scattered rice and wheat with plague-infected fleas over cities in China. It hoped to disrupt the country with a plague epidemic. It didn't work, however. After the war, the United States and the Soviet Union reportedly researched plague as a weapon. Both countries may have developed methods for spreading plague without fleas. Today, most countries have stopped their bioweapons programs.

Reports of current outbreaks of the plague may be frightening. But outbreaks are rare and generally involve only a few cases. Now that scientists understand what the plague is and how to treat it, it is unlikely that the world will be devastated by another plague pandemic.

STRAIGHT TO THE
SOURCE

Journalist Kaitlin Sullivan reported on an outbreak of the bubonic plague in California in the summer of 2020:

> *A California man was confirmed to have contracted the plague earlier this week. . . . The man, a South Lake Tahoe resident, was California's first case of plague in five years. . . . In July, Colorado also saw its first case in five years when a southwestern region resident, who has since recovered, was infected. . . . Navajo County public health officials documented a case in Arizona [in] late July. And two cases this year were reported in New Mexico, including a man who died.*
>
> *Reports of plague may sound scary, but experts say the bacterial infection is not something to fret about.*

> Source: Kaitlin Sullivan. "California Confirms First Human Case of the Plague in 5 Years: What to Know." *NBC News*, 19 Aug. 2020, nbcnews.com. Accessed 21 Apr. 2021.

POINT OF VIEW

After reading this quote, read the primary source from Chapter One about the Black Death. Each author has a different point of view on bubonic plague outbreaks. How are they different and why? How are they similar and why?

IMPORTANT DATES

541
The Justinian Plague begins. This is the first reliably recorded bubonic plague pandemic.

1347
The bubonic plague reaches Italy. It begins the pandemic in Europe now known as the Black Death.

1665
The Great Plague of London begins. About 70,000 Londoners die before the epidemic ends in 1666.

1850s
The Manchurian or Modern Plague begins. This is the final bubonic plague pandemic.

1894
Scientists discover the bacterium that causes the bubonic plague. It is later named *Yersinia pestis*.

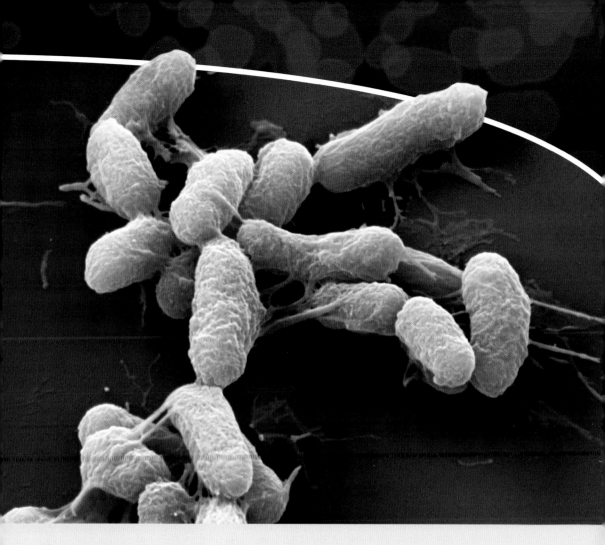

1900
The bubonic plague reaches the United States through a ship docked in San Francisco.

1924
The last outbreak of plague in an urban area of the United States occurs in Los Angeles.

2020
California has its first human case of plague in five years.

STOP AND
THINK

Tell the Tale

Chapter Three describes various explanations for the plague before scientists discovered the bacteria that cause it. Imagine you are living in the Middle Ages and don't know what this terrible illness is. What explanation might you come up with? Write 200 words about your explanation.

Dig Deeper

After reading this book, what questions do you still have about the bubonic plague? With an adult's help, find a few reliable sources that can help you answer your questions. Write a paragraph about what you learned.

Say What?

Studying the bubonic plague can mean learning a lot of new vocabulary. Find five words in this book you've never heard before. Use a dictionary to find out what they mean. Then write the meanings in your own words and use each word in a new sentence.

Why Do I Care?

Chapter Two discusses several plague pandemics of the past. But we can still learn from things that happened long ago. How did people react to pandemics in the past? What changes came about because of those pandemics? How do past disease outbreaks compare with modern ones?

GLOSSARY

bacterium
a microscopic one-celled organism; some bacteria cause infectious diseases

biologist
a scientist who studies living things and how they work

bioweapon
a harmful biological agent, such as a germ, used as a weapon

DNA
the molecule that carries genes; short for *deoxyribonucleic acid*

endemic
a disease that is consistently present in a certain area or in a certain population

epidemic
the wide spread of a disease in an area

lymph nodes
small structures that are part of the body's immune system and filter bacteria and other infectious agents

pandemic
a disease outbreak that spreads to many countries

vaccines
medicines that cause people to produce antibodies that protect them against a specific disease

ONLINE RESOURCES

To learn more about the bubonic plague, visit our free resource websites below.

Visit **abdocorelibrary.com** or scan this QR code for free Common Core resources for teachers and students, including vetted activities, multimedia, and booklinks, for deeper subject comprehension.

Visit **abdobooklinks.com** or scan this QR code for free additional online weblinks for further learning. These links are routinely monitored and updated to provide the most current information available.

LEARN MORE

Borgert-Spaniol, Megan. *Your Amazing Immune System*. Abdo, 2021.

Gagne, Tammy. *Smallpox*. Abdo, 2022.

Moon, Walt K. *Past Pandemics and COVID-19*. BrightPoint, 2021.

INDEX

antibiotics, 36–37

bioweapons, 40
Black Death, 8–9, 11, 14, 16–18, 19, 20, 29
Boccaccio, Giovanni, 11
buboes, 8, 18, 29

diagnosis, 10, 33, 34–37
doctors, 10, 18, 23, 26, 34

epidemic, 6, 14, 18, 38, 40

face masks, 29

Justinian Plague, 14–15

lymph nodes, 8, 28, 34

Modern Plague, 20–21, 29

pandemic, 8–9, 14–15, 16–18, 20–21, 23, 29, 40
Petrarch, 20
pneumonic plague, 29, 30–31, 34, 37

scientists, 8, 14, 21, 23–24, 40

septicemic plague, 29, 34
Shibasaburo, Kitasato, 24
Sullivan, Kaitlin, 41
symptoms, 5, 6, 8, 13, 16, 28–31

vaccines, 37

World Health Organization (WHO), 9, 37

Yersin, Alexandre, 24
Yersinia pestis, 7, 24

zoonosis, 9

About the Author

Yvette LaPierre lives in North Dakota with her family and advises students in the Indians Into Medicine Program and at the University of North Dakota. She writes and edits books and articles for children and adults.